THE ROCK CYCLE

REBECCA FELIX

Consulting Editor, Diane Craig, M.A./Reading Specialist

Sandcastle

An Imprint of Abdo Publishing
abdopublishing.com

abdopublishing.com

Published by Abdo Publishing, a division of ABDO, PO Box 398166, Minneapolis, Minnesota 55439. Copyright © 2018 by Abdo Consulting Group, Inc. International copyrights reserved in all countries. No part of this book may be reproduced in any form without written permission from the publisher. SandCastle™ is a trademark and logo of Abdo Publishing.

Printed in the United States of America, North Mankato, Minnesota

102017
012018

Design: Kelly Doudna, Mighty Media, Inc.
Production: Mighty Media, Inc.
Editor: Liz Salzmann
Cover Photographs: iStockphoto, Shutterstock
Interior Photographs: iStockphoto, Shutterstock, Wikimedia Commons

Publisher's Cataloging-in-Publication Data

Names: Felix, Rebecca, author.
Title: The rock cycle / by Rebecca Felix.
Description: Minneapolis, Minnesota : Abdo Publishing, 2018. | Series: Our extreme earth |
Identifiers: LCCN 2017946509 | ISBN 9781532112256 (lib.bdg.) |
        ISBN 9781614799672 (ebook)
Subjects: LCSH: Petrology--Juvenile literature. | Geochemical cycles--Juvenile literature. |
        Earth sciences--Juvenile literature.
Classification: DDC 552--dc23
LC record available at https://lccn.loc.gov/2017946509

SandCastle™ Level: Fluent

SandCastle™ books are created by a team of professional educators, reading specialists, and content developers around five essential components—phonemic awareness, phonics, vocabulary, text comprehension, and fluency—to assist young readers as they develop reading skills and strategies and increase their general knowledge. All books are written, reviewed, and leveled for guided reading, early reading intervention, and Accelerated Reader® programs for use in shared, guided, and independent reading and writing activities to support a balanced approach to literacy instruction. The SandCastle™ series has four levels that correspond to early literacy development. The levels are provided to help teachers and parents select appropriate books for young readers.

EMERGING · BEGINNING · TRANSITIONAL · FLUENT

CONTENTS

ABOUT THE ROCK CYCLE

Rocks are found all over Earth.
How do they form?

Some begin with
volcanoes.

Volcanoes push out **magma**.
It cools and hardens.

It becomes **igneous** rock.

Weather breaks the rock into small pieces.

Erosion does too. Wind and water move the pieces.

Over time, **layers** of dirt cover the rocks. This presses on the rocks.

The pieces stick together. They become **sedimentary** rock.

The rock gets buried under more **layers** of dirt.

It is very hot underground. The heat changes the rocks.

They become different kinds of
metamorphic rocks.

For example, they
can become slate
or marble.

Some rocks end up very deep underground. There, it is so hot the rocks melt.

They become **magma**. Then the rock **cycle** begins again.

James Hutton was a **petrologist**.
He studied rocks on his farm.

He was the first to say that rocks
form in a **cycle**.

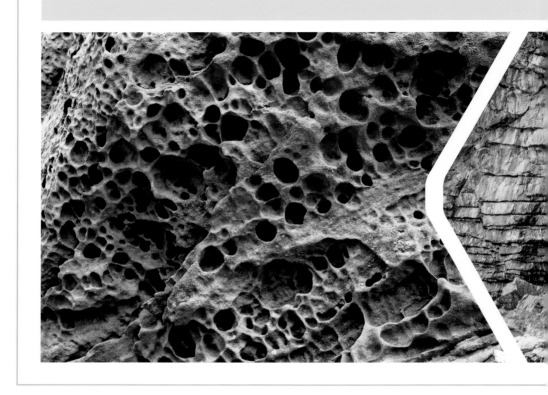

People use the rock **cycle** to understand history.

It teaches us about Earth.

THINK ABOUT IT

There are many kinds of rocks.
What rocks can you find near you?

GLOSSARY

cycle – a series of events that happen over and over again.

erosion – wearing away of the land often caused by water or wind.

igneous – created from cooled magma.

layer – one thickness of a material or a substance lying over or under another.

magma – melted rock below Earth's surface.

metamorphic – changed by pressure and heat.

petrologist – a scientist who studies the origin, history, structure, content, and classification of rocks.

sedimentary – created from rock pieces moved by water or wind.